Just Kidding!

Monster Laughs

By Paul Virr

Illustrated by Amanda Enright
and Kasia Dudziuk

WINDMILL BOOKS

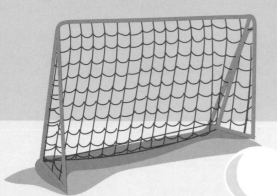

Published in 2020 by Windmill Books,
an Imprint of Rosen Publishing
29 East 21st Street, New York, NY 10010

Cataloging-in-Publication Data

Names: Virr, Paul.
Title: Monster laughs / Paul Virr.
Description: New York : Windmill Books, 2020. | Series: Just kidding! | Includes glossary and index.
Identifiers: ISBN 9781538391242 (pbk.) | ISBN 9781538391266 (library bound) | ISBN 9781538391259 (6 pack)
Subjects: LCSH: Monsters--Juvenile humor. | Ghosts--Juvenile humor. | Wit and humor, Juvenile. | Riddles, Juvenile.
Classification: LCC PN6231.M665 V577 2019 | DDC 818'.602 --dc23

Manufactured in the United States of America

CPSIA Compliance Information: Batch BS19WM: For Further Information contact Rosen Publishing, New York, New York at 1-800-237-9932

Contents

Fang-tastically Funny!

Why do vampires chew gum? Because they have bat breath!

What type of dog does a vampire have? A bloodhound!

What goes "baa!" and has two sharp fangs?
A lamb-pire!

Which fruit do vampires love the best?
Neck-tarines!

Vampire School

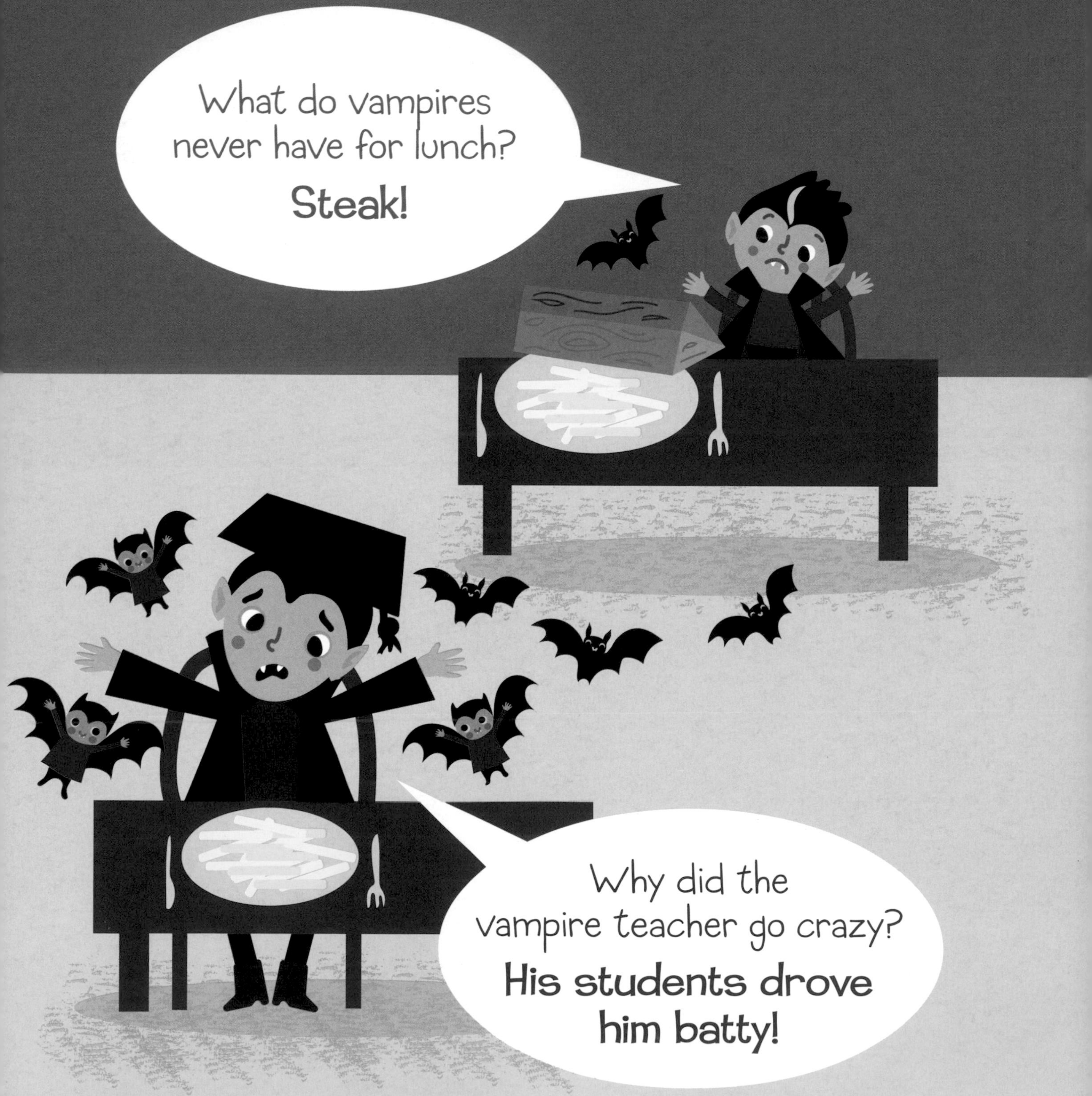

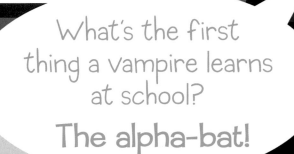

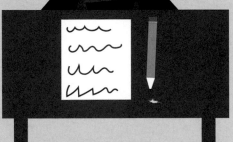

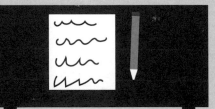

Munching Monsters

Why are vampires always hungry?
Because they eat necks to nothing!

What do monsters have for dessert?
Ice-scream!

How do monsters like their eggs?
Terror-fried!
What does the Abominable Snowman eat for breakfast?
Frosted flakes!

Going Batty!

What do vampire bats do when they meet up?
They just hang out!

BANK
Why did the mean vampire have no friends?
Because he was a pain in the neck!

BANK
What does a vampire say if you give it a present?
Fangs a lot!

Monster Party!

What do you call a vampire that's always hungry?
Snack-ula!

Which monster is always playing tricks on people?
Prank-enstein!

Which soup does
a vampire eat?
Scream of tomato!

Which party game
do ghosts play?
Hide-and-shriek!

Wacky Werewolves

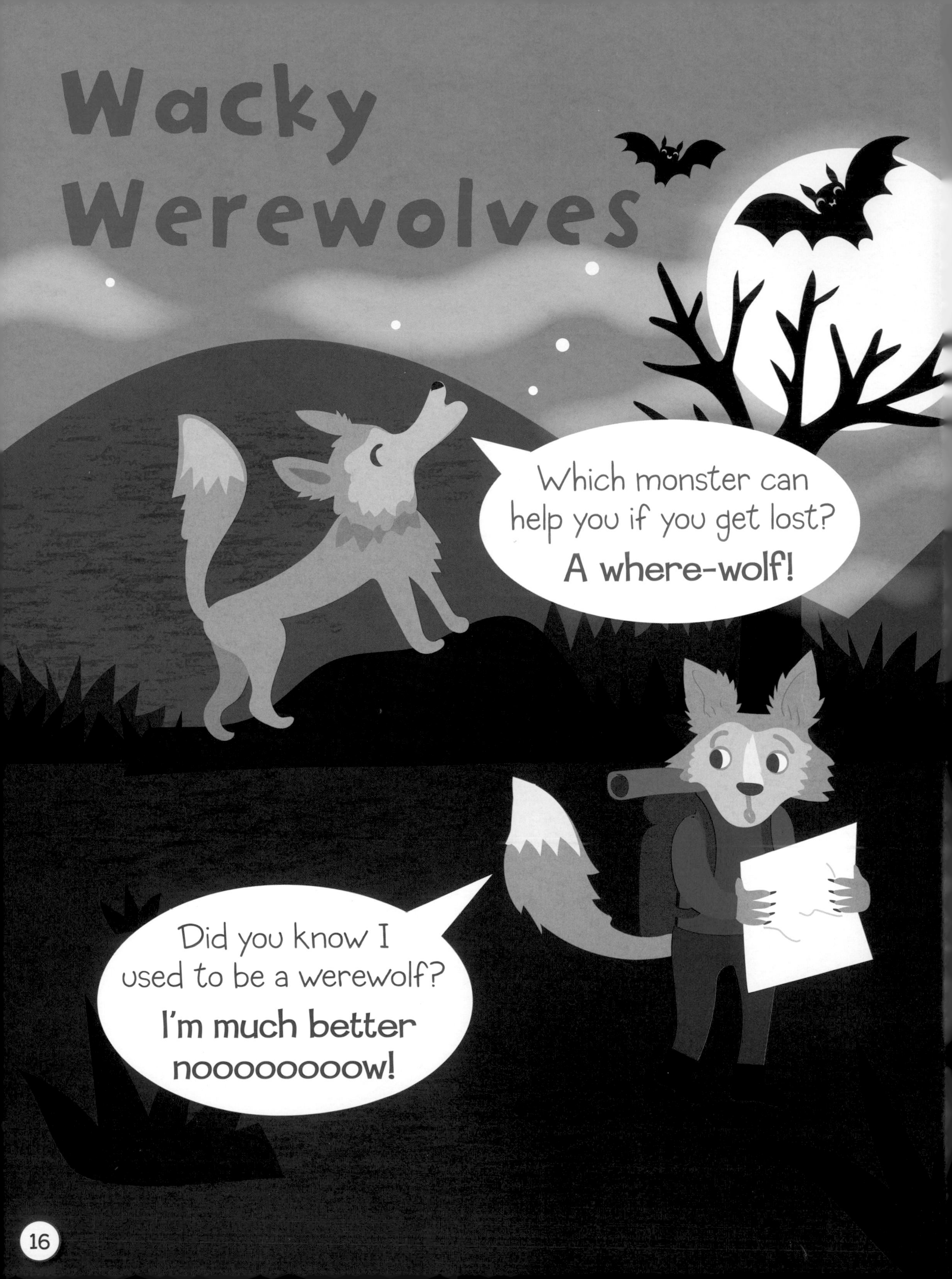

Why do werewolves never eat clowns? They taste funny!
What do you get if you cross a hyena with a werewolf? I don't know, but if it starts laughing, you'd better join in!

Silly Spells

What do you call a nervous witch?

A twitch!

Did you hear about the twin witches?

Nobody knew which witch was which!

What does the world's fastest witch ride? A vroomstick!

Why was the witch at the top of her class? Because she was good at spelling!

Monsters on the Move

What do you call a witch with a broken broom?

A witch-hiker!

What do you call a huge monster in a small car?
Stuck!

Why did the ghost catch the train? Because it loved to travel by wail!

Monstrously Funny!

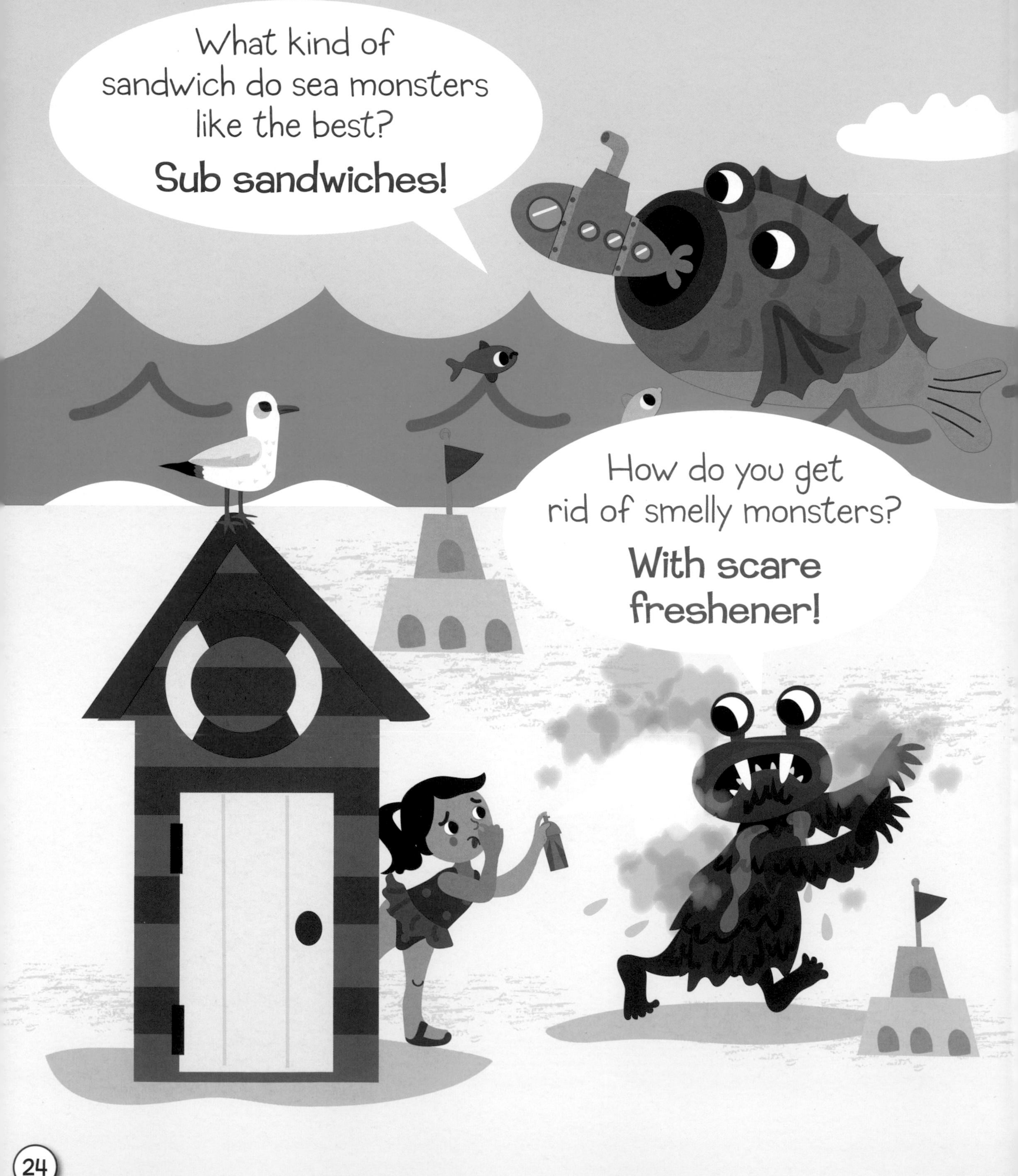

Why did the monster eat a lamp? **She needed a light snack!**

What should you do if a monster sits on your bicycle? **Get a new bicycle!**

Sick Monster Jokes

How do you know when a vampire has caught a cold?
He keeps coffin!

Did you hear about the witch who caught a cold?
The doctor told her to stay in bed for a spell.

What did the vampire doctor say to her patients?
Necks, please!
How did the monster stop her nose from running?
She stuck out her foot and tripped it!

Scary Sports Day

Who won the vampires' running race? It was a draw—they all finished neck and neck!

Which sport does a giant, big-footed monster play? Squash!

What's big, scary, and has four wheels?
A monster on a skateboard.

Which sport are vampires best at playing?
Bat-minton!

It's Snow Joke!

What do you get if you cross the Abominable Snowman with a crocodile?

Frostbite!

How does the Abominable Snowman relax?

He just chills out!

What's on top of the Abominable Snowman's bed?
A blanket of snow!

How does the Abominable Snowman score a goal?
With a snowball!

Glossary

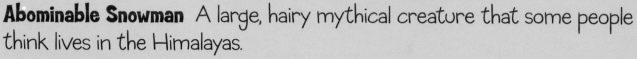

Abominable Snowman A large, hairy mythical creature that some people think lives in the Himalayas.

bloodhound A breed of dog with a very strong sense of smell.

Frankenstein A monster in the shape of a man, from a story called Frankenstein.

frostbite Damage to the body caused by freezing.

vampire In stories, a dead person who is believed to rise at night to suck the blood of living people.

werewolf In stories, a person who can transform into a wolf.

Index